Canada

Canada

Production de l'Office national du film du Canada
Service de la photographie
Ottawa
En collaboration avec Clarke, Irwin & Company Limited
Toronto, Vancouver

Produced by the National Film Board of Canada
Still Photography Division
Ottawa
In association with Clarke, Irwin & Company Limited
Toronto, Vancouver

© 1973 National Film Board of Canada/l'Office national du film du Canada

ISBN 07720 0695 4

Printed in Canada / Imprimé au Canada

© 1973 National Film Board of Canada/l'Office national du film du Canada

ISBN 07720 0695 4

Printed in Canada / Imprimé au Canada

Canada

As the waters grey grace meets you
but only in gulls that hook on the wind
are shaken easily loose
curve to the curving wave

Not these the mark of Canada
nor yet the sentry beat of bergs
around the fading palaces
of fog your ship salutes
but here where heads of Hebridean mould
toss in crusted dories hard Saxon fingers
sift dour living from the drowned
and drowning Banks

Earle Birney *from*
MARITIME FACES

LES OISEAUX de mer ne regardent pas la mer
ils volent pour un heureux voyage
et prolongent dans la nuit un désir inconnu
au-delà des mers
et s'engloutissent la tête qui pointe
remplis de soleil et d'obscurité légère
les oiseaux de mer ne regardent pas la mer

Gabriel Charpentier

LES OISEAUX DE MER

And all around me the thin light,
So sere, so melancholy bright,
Fell like the half-reflected gleam
Or shadow of some former dream;
A moment's golden reverie
Poured out on every plant and tree
A semblance of weird joy, or less,
A sort of spectral happiness;
And I, too, standing idly there,
With muffled hands in the chill air,
Felt the warm glow about my feet,
and shuddering betwixt cold and heat,
Drew my thoughts closer, like a cloak,
While something in my blood awoke,
A nameless and unnatural cheer,
A pleasure secret and austere.

Archibald Lampman *from*

IN NOVEMBER

Dans la lumière leur feuillage est comme l'eau
Des îles d'eau claire
Sur le noir de l'épinette ombrée à contre-jour

Saint-Denys-Garneau
PINS À CONTRE-JOUR

Outward the sun explodes light
like a mild rehearsal of light to come
over the vitreous waters
At this edge of the blast
a young girl sits on a granite bench
so still as if already only
silhouette burned in the stone.

Earle Birney *from*

NOVEMBER WALK NEAR FALSE CREEK MOUTH

Ma langue est d'Amérique

Je suis né de ce paysage

J'ai pris souffle dans le limon du fleuve

Je suis la terre et je suis la parole

Le soleil se lève à la plante de mes pieds

Le soleil s'endort sous ma tête

Mes bras sont deux océans le long de mon corps

Le monde entier vient frapper à mes flancs

Gatien Lapointe *tiré de*

ODE AU SAINT-LAURENT

The sea retains such images
in her ever-changing waves;
for all her infinite variety, and the forms,
inexhaustible, of her loves,
she is constant always in beauty,
which to us need be nothing more
than a harmony with the wave on which we move.
All ugliness is a distortion
of the lovely lines and curves
which sincerity makes out of hands
and bodies moving in air.
Beauty is ordered in nature
as the wind and sea
shape each other for pleasure; as the just
know, who learn of happiness
from the report of their own actions.

Louis Dudek *from*
EUROPE, 1954

Mais il suffit peut-être
O Terre
De gratter légèrement ta surface
Avec des doigts d'innocence
Avec des doigts de soleil

Alain Grandbois

LE SILENCE

Vast and immaculate! No pilgrim bands,
In ecstasy before the Parian shrines,
Knew such a temple built by human hands,
With this transcendent rhythm in its lines;
Like an epic on the North Atlantic stream
It moved, and fairer than a Phidian dream.

Rich gifts unknown to kings were duly brought
At dawn and sunset and at cloudless noons,
Gifts from the sea-gods and the sun who wrought
Cascades and rainbows; flung them in festoons
Over the spires, with emerald, amethyst,
Sapphire and pearl out of their fiery mist.

And music followed when a litany,
Begun with the ring of foam bells and the purl
Of linguals as the edges cut the sea,
Crashed upon a rising storm with whirl
Of floes from far-off spaces where Death rides
The darkened belfries of his evening tides.

Within the sunlight, vast, immaculate!
Beyond all reach of earth in majesty,
It passed on southwards slowly to its fate–
To be drawn down by the inveterate sea
Without one chastening fire made to start
From alters built around its polar heart.

E. J. Pratt
THE SEA-CATHEDRAL

Nous sommes sans limites
Et l'abondance est notre mère.
Pays ceinturé d'acier
Aux grands yeux de lacs
A la bruissante barbe résineuse
Je te salue et je salue ton rire de chutes.
Pays casqué de glaces polaires
Auréolé d'aurores boréales
Et tendant aux générations futures
L'étincelante garbe de tes feux d'uranium.
Nous lançons contre ceux qui te pillent et t'épuisent
Contre ceux que parasitent sur ton grand corps d'humus et de neige
Les imprécations foudroyantes
Qui naissent aux gorges des orages.

Gilles Hénault *tiré de*

JE TE SALUE

Come to me
Not as a river willingly downward falls
To be lost in a wide ocean
But come to me
As flood-tide comes to shore-line
Filling empty bays
With a white stillness
Mating earth and sea.

F. R. Scott

UNION

Abandonne-toi à la mer,
Laisse-la te sculpter à son image,
Te polir de son éternelle patience.

Simone Routier *tiré de*
LE DIVIN ANÉANTISSEMENT

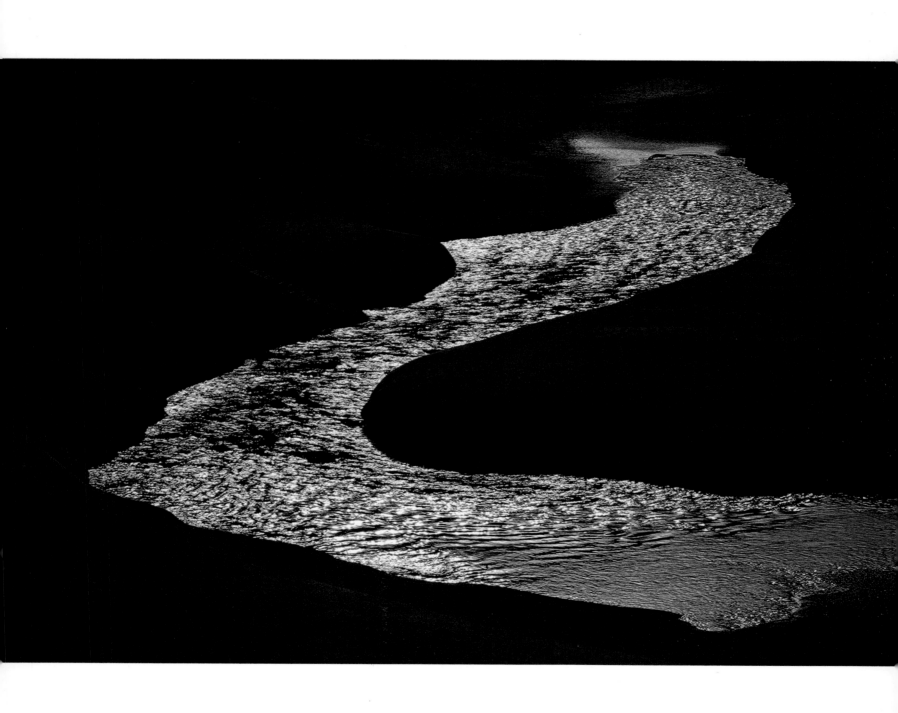

The dust, light brown,
lightens as it sifts thru eyebrows
on the face you see
looking to the prairie wind.

George Bowering *from*
THE DUST

Femme aux couleurs de mon pays
Ne vois-tu pas mes castors qui s'acharnent
A défaire les mailles des saisons
En opposant des digues à l'hiver
Pour retenir les larmes de ces lacs si beaux
Que pleure mon amour sur toi sur mon pays

Ne sens-tu pas des Laurentides aux Rocheuses
Les doigts du vent viril avides de peigner
Tes longs cheveux de blé au front de tes prairies

N'entends-tu pas venir la vaste chevauchée
Des nuages bruyants que l'amour éperonne
Avant d'éclabousser les chairs les plus fertiles
En piétinant ton ciel de sabots de tonnerre

Pierre Trottier *tiré de*
FEMME AUX COULEURS DE MON PAYS

This is a beauty
of dissonance,
this resonance
of stony strand,
this smoky cry
curled over a black pine
like a broken
and wind-battered branch
when the wind
bends the tops of the pines
and curdles the sky
from the north.

This is the beauty
of strength
broken by strength
and still strong.

A. J. M. Smith *from*
THE LONELY LAND

La neige nous met en rêve sur de vastes plaines, sans
traces ni couleur

Veille mon coeur, la neige nous met en selle sur des
coursiers d'écume

Sonne l'enfance couronnée, la neige nous sacre en
haute mer, plein songe, toutes voiles dehors

La neige nous met en magie, blancheur étale, plumes
gonflées où perce l'oeil rouge de cet oiseau

Mon coeur; trait de feu sous des palmes de gel file
le sang qui s'émerveille.

Anne Hébert

NEIGE

The wind plays strange pranks with snow;
snow is the most plastic medium it has to mould
into images and symbols of its moods. Here
one of these promontories would slope down,
and the very next one would slope upward as it
advanced across the open space. In every case
there had been two walls, as it were, of
furious blow, and between the two a lane of compar-
ative calm, caused by the shelter of a clump of
brush or weeds, in which the snow had taken
refuge from the wind's rough and savage play.

Frederick Philip Grove *from*

OVER PRAIRIE TRAILS

De mon grand pays solitaire
Je crie avant que de me taire
A tous les hommes de la terre
Ma maison c'est votre maison
Entre mes quatre murs de glace
Je mets mon temps et mon espace
A préparer le feu la place
Pour les humains de l'horizon
Et les humains sont de ma race

Gilles Vigneault *tiré de*
MON PAYS

Here clove the keels of centuries ago
Where now unvisited the flats lie bare.
Here seethed the sweep of journeying waters, where
No more the tumbling floods of Fundy flow,
And only in the samphire pipes creep slow
The salty currents of the sap. The air
Hums desolately with wings that seaward fare,
Over the lonely reaches beating low.

The wastes of hard and meagre weeds are thronged
With murmurs of a past that time has wronged;
And ghosts of many an ancient memory
Dwell by the brackish pools and ditches blind,
In these low-lying pastures of the wind,
These marshes pale and meadows by the sea.

Charles G. D. Roberts

THE SALT FLATS

Il faut que le fleuve se poursuive, à perte de vue,
à perte de vue même pour les aveugles. Un lit n'a pas
de limites. Un fleuve ne connaît pas de frontières.
Et l'on retrouve sur les rives, au printemps, quelques
belles chevelures noyées par le courant, quelques lèvres
couvertes encore d'écume, quelques boucles d'oreilles
devenues coquillages séchés.

En certains milieux on dit que c'est la rançon, ailleurs,
à voix basse, on répète une chanson.

Et tout continue. Continuellement.

Roland Giguère

YEUX FIXES

I fear continually that the premature night
Will hunt me down darkly one noon,
That time will betray me and I'll fall
And with lips attuned to earth
I shall drink as though I had never known
The pit of isolation.
Surrounded by the unremembered calm
Of gentle hills and patient vegetation
I shall forget the horror of the earth.
Softly the whisper of abundant rose
Blooming like starfish
Will mingle with my flesh.
The melancholy pines
Coerce the landscape.

Waclaw Iwaniuk

I FEAR CONTINUALLY THAT THE PREMATURE NIGHT

L'hiver viendra laver la terre.
Et, sur les meubles du printemps,
On posera, la main légère,
Des pots de fleurs dans tous les champs.

Éloi de Grandmont *tiré de*

LE VOYAGE D'ARLEQUIN

The world is my country
The human race is my race
The spirit of man is my God
The future of man is my heaven

F. R. Scott

CREED

Eh bien! je boirai tant les souffles d'aventure,
Je ferai tant chanter dans mes jeunes poumons
La respiration de la forte nature,
Que ma voix bondira sur le sommet des monts.

Robert Choquette *tiré de*

VIVRE ET CRÉER

Les remerciements

Nous avons une dette de reconnaissance envers les auteurs, et les maisons d'édition suivantes, qui nous ont permis de puiser dans leurs oeuvres les textes de ce volume: Gabriel Charpentier pour 'Les Oiseaux de Mer'; les Editions Fides pour 'Pins à contre-jour' de Saint-Denys-Garneau; Gatien Lapointe et les Editions du Jour, pour un passage de 'Ode au Saint-Laurent'; Alain Grandbois et les Editions de l'Hexagone pour 'Le Silence'; Gilles Hénault et les Editions de l'Hexagone, pour un extrait de 'Je te salue'; Simone Routier pour un passage de 'Le divin anéantissement'; Pierre Trottier et les Editions de l'Hexagone, pour un passage de 'Femme aux couleurs de mon pays'; Anne Hébert et les Editions du Seuil pour 'Neige' (*Poèmes*, 1960); Gilles Vigneault et les Editions de l'Arc, pour un passage de 'Mon Pays'; Roland Giguère et les Editions de l'Hexagone pour 'Yeux fixes'; Eloi de Grandmont pour un passage de 'Le voyage d'Arlequin'; Robert Choquette et les Editions Fides pour un passage de 'Vivre et créer'.

Acknowledgments

We acknowledge with gratitude: Earle Birney and McClelland & Stewart Limited, Toronto for the excerpts from 'November Walk near False Creek Mouth' and 'Maritime Faces' (*Selected Poems*, 1966); Archibald Lampman for an excerpt from 'In November' (*Selected Poems of Archibald Lampman*, 1947); Louis Dudek for an excerpt from 'Europe, 1954'; F. R. Scott for 'Creed' and 'Union'; George Bowering and McClelland & Stewart Limited, Toronto for an excerpt from 'The Dust' (*Rocky Mountain Foot*, 1968); A. J. M. Smith and Oxford University Press (Canadian Branch) for an excerpt from 'The Lonely Land' (*Poems, New & Collected*, 1967); A. Leonard Grove for the excerpt from *Over Prairie Trails* by Frederick Philip Grove (1922, 1957); Lady Roberts for 'The Salt Flats' by Charles G. D. Roberts (*Selected Poems*, 1955); Waclaw Iwaniuk and the Sono Nis Press for an excerpt from 'I Fear Continually that the Premature Night' (*Volvox*, 1971). 'The Sea-Cathedral' by E. J. Pratt is reprinted from *Collected Poems* by E. J. Pratt (1958), with the permission of The Macmillan Company of Canada Limited.

Maquette et choix des photos	Design and Photo Editing
LORRAINE MONK	LORRAINE MONK
ALLAN FLEMING	ALLAN FLEMING
ERNIE HERZIG	ERNIE HERZIG

Choix des poèmes	Poetry Selections
MICHAEL GNAROWSKI	MICHAEL GNAROWSKI

Légendes	Captions
JOHN DE VISSER	JOHN DE VISSER

Assistantes à la production	Production Assistants
MADELEINE MURPHY	MADELEINE MURPHY
EDNA VARRIN	EDNA VARRIN

Recherche photographique	Photo Research
MARJORIE TRIM	MARJORIE TRIM

Les photographes	The photographers
KENNETH C. ALEXANDER	KENNETH C. ALEXANDER
PAUL BAICH	PAUL BAICH
EGON BORK	EGON BORK
PETER D'ANGELO	PETER D'ANGELO
JOHN DE VISSER	JOHN DE VISSER
LUTZ DILLE	LUTZ DILLE
JOHN FOSTER	JOHN FOSTER
JEAN-LOUIS FRUND	JEAN-LOUIS FRUND
PENNY GODDARD	PENNY GODDARD
TED GRANT	TED GRANT
FRED HERZOG	FRED HERZOG
IRWIN KARNICK	IRWIN KARNICK
PETER KELLY	PETER KELLY
J. A. KRAULIS	J. A. KRAULIS
BRUCE LITTELJOHN	BRUCE LITTELJOHN
MALAK	MALAK
MIA ET KLAUS	MIA AND KLAUS
FREEMAN PATTERSON	FREEMAN PATTERSON
KRYN TACONIS	KRYN TACONIS
ROGER TESSIER	ROGER TESSIER
RICHARD VROOM	RICHARD VROOM
WENDY WALLICK	WENDY WALLICK
WOODS ET MATTHEWS	WOODS AND MATTHEWS

Composition à la monotype en Garamond par
Cooper & Beatty, Limited

Typography by Cooper & Beatty, Limited
in Garamond Monotype

Séparation des couleurs et impression au Protone
par Herzig Somerville Ltd, Toronto, Canada

Protone colour separations and printing by
Herzig Somerville Ltd, Toronto, Canada

Le Protone est un nouveau procédé de reproduction
en offset cinq couleurs imaginé par Herzig
Somerville Ltd. La mise au point des encres
transparentes utilisées dans ce procédé est
l'oeuvre de la Lester Inks & Chemicals Ltd, de
Toronto. Le P.A.I.T. (Programme d'avancement de
la technologie industrielle) du ministère fédéral
de l'Industrie et du Commerce, Ottawa, a
été le levier de ces recherches.

Protone is a new five colour offset
reproduction process developed by
Herzig Somerville Ltd. The Pellucid inks
used in this process were researched by
Lester Ink & Chemical Ltd Toronto. This research
was made possible with the support of P.A.I.T.
(Program for the advancement of industrial
technology) Federal Department of Industry,
Trade and Commerce, Ottawa.

Parties Texte
Domtar
Byronic Text
Gris, Grammage 160M

Text Sections
Domtar
Byronic Text
Grey, Basis 160M

Parties Couleur
Domtar
Suedetone Offset Enamel
Blanc, Grammage 240M

Colour Sections
Domtar
Suedetone Offset Enamel
White, Basis 240M

Feuilles de garde
Domtar
Byronic Text
Ultra Blanc, Grammage 160M

End Papers
Domtar
Byronic Text
Britewhite, Basis 160M

Couvre-Livre
Domtar
Luxagloss Offset Enamel
Blanc, Grammage 200M

Book Jacket
Domtar
Luxagloss Offset Enamel
White, Basis 200M

Couverture
Columbia Finishing Mills
Toile 'Bradford'

Cover Material
Columbia Finishing Mills
Bradford Linen

Reliure par
John Deyell Company

Binding by
John Deyell Company

L'édition originale de cet ouvrage fût tirée à cinq cents exemplaires pour perpétuer le souvenir de la Conférence des chefs de gouvernement du Commonwealth, qui s'est tenue à Ottawa du 2 au 10 août 1973

This book was originally produced in a limited edition of five hundred copies to commemorate the Commonwealth Heads of Government Meeting held in Ottawa, August 2 to 10, 1973

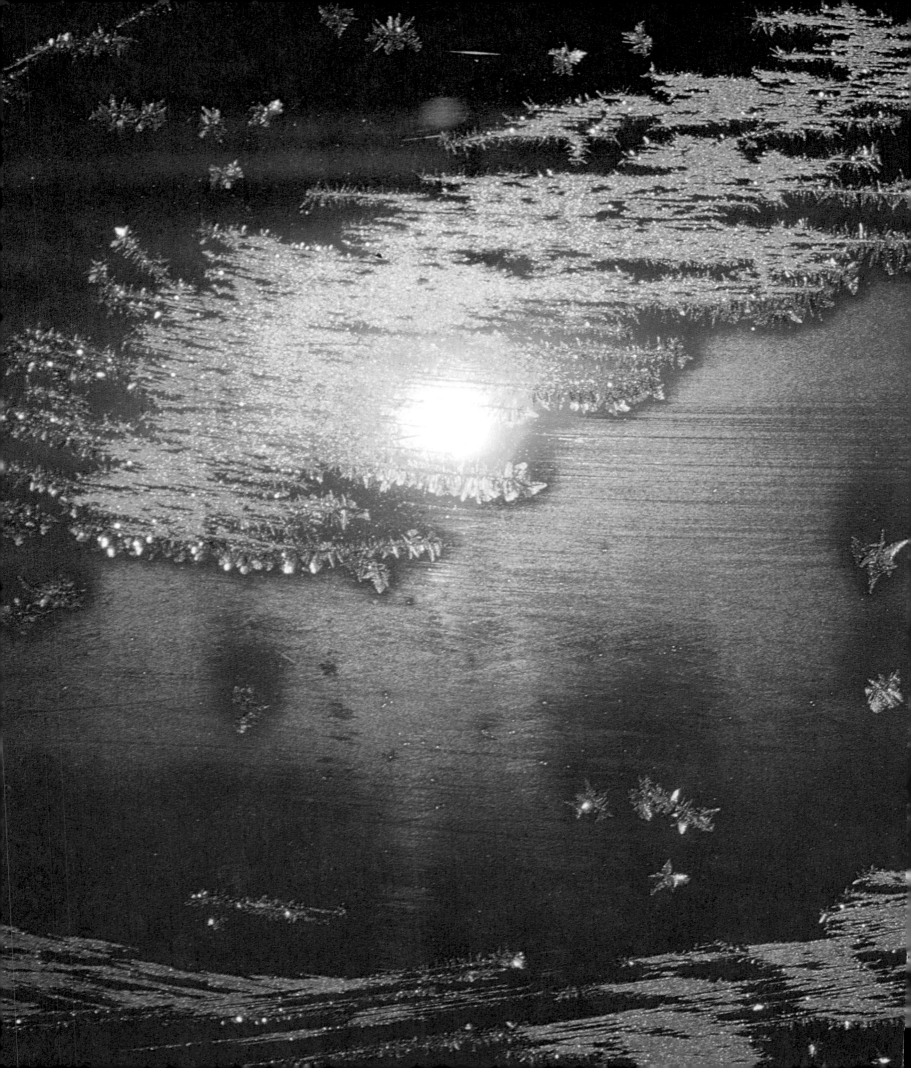